1.00

10/23

Kindness and Joy

D0925803

Kind hearts are the gardens,

Kind thoughts are the roots,

Kind words are the flowers,

Kind deeds are the fruits.

Take care of your garden,

And keep out the weeds.

Fill it with sunshine,

Kind words and kind deeds.

—Henry W. Longfellow

Kindness and Joy

Expressing the Gentle Love

HAROLD G. KOENIG, M.D.

Templeton Foundation Press

Philadelphia & London

Templeton Foundation Press
300 Conshohocken State Road, Suite 670
West Conshohocken, PA 19428
www.templetonpress.org

© 2006 by Harold G. Koenig

All rights reserved. No part of this book may be used or reproduced,
stored in a retrieval system, or transmitted in any form or by any means,
electronic, mechanical, photocopying, recording, or otherwise,
without the written permission of Templeton Foundation Press.

*Templeton Foundation Press helps intellectual leaders and others learn
about science research on aspects of realities, invisible and intangible.
Spiritual realities include unlimited love, accelerating creativity, worship,
and the benefits of purpose in persons and in the cosmos.*

Unless otherwise noted, scripture taken from the HOLY BIBLE, NEW INTERNA-
TIONAL VERSION®. Copyright © 1973, 1978, 1984 by International Bible Society.
Used by permission of Zondervan Publishing House. All rights reserved. The "NIV"
and "New International Version" trademarks are registered in the United States
Patent and Trademark Office by the International Bible Society. Use of either
trademark requires the permission of International Bible Society.

Library of Congress Cataloging-in-Publication Data

Koenig, Harold George.
Kindness and joy : expressing the gentle love / Harold G. Koenig.
p.   cm.
Includes bibliographical references.
ISBN-13: 978-1-59947-106-8 (pbk. : alk. paper)
ISBN-10: 1-59947-106-X (pbk. : alk. paper)
1. Kindness. 2. Charity. 3. Joy. I. Title.

BJ1533.K5K64 2006
177'.7—dc22   2006017798

Designed and typeset by Helene Krasney
Printed in the United States of America
06 07 08 09 10 11   10 9 8 7 6 5 4 3 2 1

To my wife, Charmin Marie Koenig

Contents

Introduction

Saying kind words that are truthful and sincere and putting those words into action is a sure way to experience joy. What kindness is, how to act kindly, and the emotional and spiritual benefits of kindness are the subject of this book. If you have specific people in your life toward whom you want to be kinder, or if you simply wish to be kinder in general to those around you and are having trouble doing that consistently, then this book is for you.

As a medical physician and psychiatrist for several decades, I have taken care of a lot of people who are suffering and in great need. As a result, I have had many opportunities to practice being kind, some of which I have responded to and others to which I have not. I am an emotionally sensitive person myself, and that has often been a benefit, especially when trying to understand others' feelings. I believe it has made me a better doctor and counselor. Being emotionally sensitive, though, has also been a source of much pain for me. That experience with emotional pain allows me to speak with authority on a topic like kindness. Finally, I am a Christian, and the Bible I read calls me to be kind toward others. I want to be more consistently faithful to that calling.

When I have acted with kindness, out of genuine interest in the welfare of others, I have experienced joy and fulfillment. That may be why I enjoy my work so much, because I have so many chances to be kind to people in desperate circumstances. Despite knowing the joy that kindness brings, I am not always kind. I am impatient, easily frustrated, and often temperamental. Many times I have acted in an unkind manner to patients, friends, colleagues, and family members. During these times, I have experienced an emotion quite different from joy. It is a feeling I don't like, one that is rooted in hurt, disappointment, anger, pride, and fearful self-concern. It signals to me that I am not at my best.

One reason I decided to write this book was that somehow I felt it might help me become a kinder person. When I am kind, I not only feel better, but the people around me are nicer and easier to get along with. And indeed, just writing about kindness has given me a greater sense of joy, since it has motivated me to be kinder. I suspect that many of you who are reading this book are in a similar predicament. The struggle over whether to focus on one's own needs or on those of others is indeed one of the greatest challenges we all face. Over time, hopefully, we learn to be less obsessively concerned about ourselves. We realize that God will take care of us if we seek to care for his other children, who are often much worse off than we are. I suspect that this is what it really means to grow in maturity.

Please join me in this exciting journey to seek a better understanding of kindness, joy, how they are related, and how to become more habitual in acts of kindness, in the experience of joy and, even when joy is lacking, in becoming the kind of people we were created to be.

When you carry out acts of kindness you get

a wonderful feeling inside. It is as though

something inside your body responds and says,

yes, this is how I ought to feel.

—HAROLD KUSHNER

Trust in the LORD, *and do good . . .*

and he shall give thee the desires of thine heart.

—PSALM 37:3, 4

Kindness and Joy

Kindness is tenderness.

Kindness is love,

but perhaps greater than love . . .

Kindness is good will.

Kindness says, "I want you to be happy."

—RANDOLPH RAY, FOUNDER,

THE FAMILY OF THE LITTLE CHURCH

AROUND THE CORNER

Kindness—
The Gentle, Generous Love

K indness is an action and way of acting toward another. It is a gentle, caring form of love that is given by one human to another, and may include kind acts and/or kind words. Kindness involves the whole person of the giver, his or her deepest and most sincere intention. Kindness is always gentle and is often communicated with a soft touch, a warm embrace, a caring look, or an understanding smile. Kindness may involve tremendous effort and be heroic and self-sacrificing. However, it can also be very simple, like going out of one's way to be courteous, considerate, or nice to others. This form of love can be directed toward anyone at any time—strangers, friends, customers, colleagues, or family. Whether from the giver or the receiver of kindness, according to Pascal, "Kind words do not cost much. Yet they accomplish much." As an old Mayan proverb says, "One can pay back the loan of gold, but one dies forever in debt to those who are kind."

Real kindness is altruistic and generous at its core. It involves a giving of oneself to another in a completely other-centered way. Kindness is honest and up front. Kindness expects nothing in return, and is wholly focused on the other person's *good*. The kind person must intend to do good for the other.

Although kindness includes the deepest intention of the giver, it also involves more than just good intention. Kindness uses common sense. Offering to pay a person's rent when that person is capable of working and paying his or her own rent is not being kind. Encouraging someone to sit in a wheelchair so that you can push the person when he or she really needs to walk in order to gain strength is not an act of kindness.

Offering a donut to an overweight child or a drink to an alcoholic is not being kind. Although the receiver may appreciate such acts and the giver may feel good about them, the ultimate good of the receiver is not being considered. Kindness kills in these situations. Kind acts are done with forethought and consideration of the consequences, always with the good of the other person in mind. Benjamin Disraeli said, "The greatest good you can do for another is not just to share your riches but to reveal to him his own."

Finally, kindness shows appreciation for others' acts of kindness. In this society, everyone is intensely independent. We rely on ourselves, not on others. We don't like having others do things for us. We don't like having to depend on anyone. Kindness runs counter to this obsessive need for self-sufficiency when others offer help. We can be kind to others by allowing them to be kind to us and by showing deep gratitude in return. There is an old saying, "Love accepts what love offers."

If you haven't any charity

in your heart,

you have the worst

kind of heart trouble.

—BOB HOPE

What Kindness Is Not

If an act of kindness is done for some ulterior motive or for some neurotic need (the need for attention or appreciation), it is not kindness. When a person acts kindly toward another but expects something in return or has a hidden agenda in mind, such actions are deceptive or manipulative, not kind.

Kindness is not rushed, irritated, impatient, or bossy. Kindness does not communicate to the receiver that the giver is being put out or imposed upon. This neutralizes the effects of kindness, both for giver and receiver. However, kindness doesn't always have to take a lot of time. What is important is the attitude and demeanor of the giver.

Kindness is not blind. Because kindness is not self-centered, kindness always seeks to learn what the needs of the other person are before it acts. It never assumes to know. Kindness always takes time to get direction from the other person. Kindness asks, "What are your needs and how can I help?" Kindness takes time to listen and hear what the person is saying, and then seeks to meet his or her true need. In some circumstances, the kindest thing to do is to do nothing. As the saying goes, "Never miss an opportunity to make others happy, even if you have to leave them alone in order to do it."

Kindness is not allowing another person to push us around or to step on us. Kindness is a voluntary act in which one person chooses to give preference to another—not an act resulting from the receiver imposing his or her will on the giver or otherwise pressuring the giver. Kindness must always be freely given, never coerced. Kindness is not at all inconsistent with standing up for one's rights as a person created in God's image and deserving of respect. Kindness is not being passive and allowing others to do whatever they wish whenever they wish. In fact, allowing others to abuse or show disrespect is not being kind to them at all, since they need to have feedback on their behavior to learn that such behavior is wrong and needs to be changed (for their ultimate good). Being afraid to give such feedback is far from wanting the best and highest good for others. Kindness is not performing acts of good because one is fearful of not doing so, since the acts are motivated by the desire to relieve anxiety or fear. These actions involve self-centered motivations rather than a desire for the other person's good, which, as pointed out earlier, must be the central and only motive of the kind person. True kindness, like love, is incompatible with fear and other negative emotions.

When kindness has left people,

even for a few moments,

we become afraid of them

as if their reason had left them.

When it has left a place

where we have always found it,

it is like a shipwreck;

we drop from security

into something malevolent

and bottomless.

—WILLA CATHER

The Opposite of Kindness

To better understand what kindness really is, it may be helpful to try to identify what the opposite of kindness is. According to the thesaurus, other words for *kindness* include humaneness, caring, gentleness, thoughtfulness, compassion, benevolence, generosity, or consideration. Words that indicate the opposite of kindness include cruelty, harshness, or meanness, which in turn are associated with terms such as degeneration, disgrace, disservice, evil, malevolence, mercilessness, brutality, pitilessness, maliciousness, spitefulness, and vindictiveness.

Of all these terms, cruelty appears to come closest to the opposite of kindness. Kindness is being primarily interested in the other person's good, and being willing to take actions to promote that good. Cruelty does not involve doing good, but rather the opposite. Cruelty is focused on the other person's needs—not with a desire to relieve those needs, but rather to cause pain by increasing those needs or creating new ones. Unlike revenge, which seeks to obtain justice over a perceived injury by another, cruelty goes beyond this. The cruel person seeks to inflict suffering that is above and beyond what is just and fair. Cruelty also differs from torture, where the motive is to do harm to a person but there is some external goal such as obtaining a confession or useful information (not solely the pleasure of seeing the person suffer). Thus, cruelty involves both the desire to bring harm to another person and the seeking of pleasure that results from the harm that is done. If kindness is concerned with doing good, then cruelty is concerned with doing evil.

Another more superficial term associated with a lack of kindness is rudeness. The rude person allows the door to slam in your face. The rude person forces himself into your parking place. The rude person cuts in line in front of you at the grocery store. While not intended to cause suffering, rudeness communicates clearly that one person thinks his or her needs are more important than another's, and that the other person's feelings don't really matter. Although less serious and intentional than cruelty, rudeness is quite common in society today and is potentially the bigger problem. Rudeness, of course, has consequences. Baseball player Willie Davis had it right when he said, "If you step on people in this life, you're going to come back as a cockroach."

Perhaps less obvious than either cruelty or rudeness—but no less serious—is neglect. Neglect involves ignoring other people's needs despite being able to do something about them. Neglect does not intend to harm the other person and may not even involve contact with the other person. Nevertheless, one person has the power to meet a need, knows about the need,

There is no fear in love.

But perfect love drives out fear . . .

The one who fears

is not made perfect in love.

—1 JOHN 4:18

and decides that meeting that need is not worth time and attention. This involves a devaluation of the other person and his or her needs. For example, people are dying of starvation in Africa or a major hurricane has left thousands of people homeless, and I could do something about it, but . . . [followed by a litany of excuses and justifications]. Neglect (or indifference) is much more widespread than either rudeness or cruelty, so it may in fact fit even better as a descriptor of the opposite of kindness. When he was secretary general of the United Nations, Dag Hammarskjold said, "Indifference to evil is worse than evil itself, and in a free society, some are guilty, but all are responsible."

Fill us at daybreak

with your kindness,

that we may shout

for joy and gladness

all of our days.

—PSALM 89:14[1]

The Divine Love

There is little doubt that kindness plays a central role in the doctrine of the Judeo-Christian scriptures, and is repeatedly given as an example of Divine love. The word "kindness" appears fifty-nine times in the Bible, and the word "kind" appears many more times. In Psalm 102, kindness is described as a central descriptor of the personal characteristics of God himself: "Merciful and gracious is the Lord, slow to anger and abounding in kindness [verse 8] . . . For as the heavens are high above the earth so surpassing is his kindness toward those who fear him [verse 11] . . . But the kindness of the Lord is from eternity to eternity toward those who fear him [verse 17]."[2]

Jesus also emphasized kindness and love in his intimate discussions with his disciples. This was especially evident at the Last Supper on the evening before Jesus died.[3] Imagine if you knew that this would be your last day on earth and you had a final meeting with your family and friends. Wouldn't what you said during this last time with your loved ones be significant? Wouldn't you try to emphasize what would be most important for them after you left? Jesus did. During that supper, he left his disciples with this final, all-important message: "A new command I give you: Love one another. As I have loved you, so you must love one another. By this all men will know that you are my disciples, if you love one another" (John 13:34–35). When we are kind to one another—to family, friends, and strangers—we are living out this all-important final commandment that Jesus left us.

The importance of kindness to the Christian life is further emphasized by the apostle Paul, who mentions kindness eleven times in Acts, Romans, Corinthians, Galatians, Ephesians, Colossians, and Titus. He includes it among the fruits of the Holy Spirit ("But the fruit of the Spirit is love, joy, peace, patience, kindness, goodness, faithfulness, gentleness and self-control," Galatians 5:22–23), and among the key characteristics that Christians should seek after ("Therefore, as God's chosen people, holy and dearly loved, clothe yourselves with compassion, kindness, humility, gentleness and patience," Colossians 3:12).

The challenge, of course, is being kind when there are so many competing interests for our time and attention, some valid and others not. How do we decide whether something is worth our time or not? When we take the time to be kind to people, there will be less time for other things in life. We will have less time to meet personal goals that we have determined are important to us. As a Christian, I find this challenging, because from the scripture passages cited above, it is evident that making time for kindness is not an option. It is a command from our leader.

A curious thing happened as I was working on this chapter. Like other physicians, I have a pager for patients to contact me in an emergency and for colleagues who urgently need to get in touch with me. The pager is turned on day and night, and I carry it with me wherever I go. Most people leave messages on my voice mail or e-mail me for non-emergent matters. Well, a few moments ago, I was paged. I immediately returned the page. The person at the other end of the line was a 68-year-old man from another state who wanted to talk with me about the best way to share his experience with others. He said that he hadn't seen a doctor in twenty years and hadn't had health insurance for fifteen years, and that through diet, exercise, and meditation, he was in excellent health. He was in need of money to support himself and wanted advice on how he could use his experiences with spirituality and health to do so. It was not an unreasonable request.

I am sorry to say that I was not very kind to him; consequently, I didn't feel much joy or fulfillment. I told him that if everyone who wanted to talk with me paged me and I spent time giving advice, I would spend twenty-four hours, seven days a week on the phone. I did take a couple of minutes with the fellow, giving him the advice he was requesting as politely as I possibly could. But in no way, shape, or form, had I been kind to him. I had been rude. So, how do we as Christians resolve such situations? What would Jesus have done? Probably taken as much time as needed with the gentleman to answer his questions (although we don't know that for certain, since Jesus never had a pager to deal with!).

At some point from the time I determined who he was and the time that I responded to him, I decided that my time was more important than his time and that he was taking unfair advantage of me by paging me. Now there may be some truth in the latter, and probably his decision to page me was not the best choice, but it is clear to me in retrospect that my time is not more important than his time. We are both children of the same Father, valued equally. Spending a few moments on the phone with the man would not have created a problem for me and, had I been kind, I would have felt much better about it. At least I could have been less rude to him and kindly explained the appropriate way of contacting me for information. I'm probably not going to feel guilty about this for very long, because I recognize that I have limits and cannot help everyone to the extent needed without quickly becoming exhausted. But it does send a clear message to me that this is an area that I need to work on. I hope that the next person who pages me for advice will receive a kinder response. We'll see.

I'm willing to bet that you are also facing challenges of this nature based on your own unique circumstances, your desire to help, and the limitations of being human. We all have to make a decision about how important being kind to others is and to justify that decision based on the values and beliefs that we hold dear. In this process of deciding what to do, we also have to realize an obligation to be kind to ourselves ("Love your neighbor *as yourself*," Matthew 22:39). I don't think there is any question, though, that when we are kind to others, we are demonstrating the very qualities that characterize God himself and were emphasized by Jesus in perhaps the most important message that he gave to us.

Wherever there is a human being,

there is an opportunity for kindness.

—SENECA (5 B.C.–A.D. 65)

Three things in human life

are important.

The first is to be kind.

The second is to be kind.

The third is to be kind.

—HENRY JAMES

Why Kindness Is Important

Can you think of one thing that is more important than being kind? You might say, "Yes, how about being honest and straightforward when the situation demands it? What about sharing my knowledge, insights, and skills with others? What about giving money to the poor, volunteering to help out those in need, providing medical care to the needy, or serving as a missionary in far-off lands to spread the Gospel?"

Being truthful is important and can be an expression of kindness. However, often we are not that certain of all the facts involved in a situation. So, if error is possible, then it is probably better to err toward kindness, for kindness may be even more important than truth. American poet Robert Brault said,

A bit of fragrance

always clings

to the hand

that gives roses.

—CHINESE PROVERB

"Today I bent the truth to be kind, and I have no regret, for I am far surer of what is kind than I am of what is true."

Even when the kindest action is to tell the truth, and you are certain that you actually do have all the facts, there are ways of telling it that show humility on your part as well as concern for the feelings and well-being of the other person. Someone once said, "If you can't be kind, at least have the decency to be vague." Always, try to be kind and consider the feelings of others. You and everyone around you will benefit. Mark Twain said, "If we should deal out justice only, in this world, who would escape? No, it is better to be generous [kind], and in the end more profitable, for it gains gratitude for us, and love." We were born as social beings, and there is nothing we can do to change that. We all need love and kindness from others, and the only way to get it is to give it unselfishly.

Because kindness is a special form of love, what is said about love is also true for kindness. Perhaps the importance of being kind to others is nowhere emphasized more strongly than in Paul's Letter to the Corinthians:

> *If I speak in the tongues of men and of angels, but have not love [kindness], I am only a resounding gong or a clanging cymbal. If I have the gift of prophecy and can fathom all mysteries and all knowledge, and if I have a faith that can move mountains, but have not love [kindness], I am nothing. If I give all I possess to the poor and surrender my body to the flames, but have not love [kindness], I gain nothing.*
>
> (1 CORINTHIANS 13:1–3)

This means that no matter how many books I write, no matter now many papers I publish, no matter how much money I make, or how much fame I achieve in this lifetime, it will be all for *nothing* if I am not kind. That is definitely a sobering thought (especially after that last call I received on my pager!).

And it wasn't just Paul who emphasized this point. Abraham Lincoln said, "Kindness is the only service that will stand the storm of life and not wash out. It will wear well and will be remembered long after the prism of politeness or the complexion of courtesy has faded away." The bottom line: Not many things are more important than being kind. What a power each of us possesses! We can change the world by being kind to others. Let's use that power more often with everybody. Our joy may depend on it.

The little unremembered

acts of kindness and love

are the best parts

of a person's life.

—WILLIAM WORDSWORTH

Joy—The Sacred Emotion

What is joy and where does it come from? Joy is different from other positive emotions such as happiness, satisfaction, relief, and even well-being.

Joy is different from happiness, which is a transient positive emotion that is linked to circumstances. When I get a pay raise at work, when one of my children comes home from school with an "A" on his or her report card, when I learn that I've won the lottery—then I feel happy. It is difficult to experience happiness in the midst of suffering or negative life experiences, but we can experience joy in those situations.

Joy is different from satisfaction with life. Satisfaction is an enduring emotion associated with being content or not having negative or disturbing feelings. Like happiness, it is associated with positive life circumstances. It does not include the exhilarating, heaven-like feeling that is the hallmark of joy.

Joy is different from relief, which is the feeling one experiences after learning that something that is feared or upsetting has resolved with a good outcome. The lump in my wife's breast was not cancer. My daughter was not seriously injured in the car wreck. I'm not going to lose my job. Like happiness and satisfaction, relief is strongly linked with personal circumstances.

Joy differs from well-being. Well-being is an enduring sense of happiness that involves a global sense that things are well. The experience of well-being falls short of joy, because well-being is still a 100 percent earthly experience. It need not be connected to the transcendent or the spiritual or the sacred.

Joy is perhaps the purest and highest positive emotion that humans can experience. Imagine the miraculous birth of a deeply wanted first child of a couple. The baby emerges from the womb, bursts out into loud cries, and then, after lying on her mother's chest for a while, stops crying and opens her eyes, looking about quietly. The feeling that the new parents have at this moment is called joy. There is nothing else like it. Joy is special because people can experience it in the midst of difficult circumstances and may even have glimpses of joy in the midst of suffering or other negative emotions like depression.

The ultimate source of joy, I believe, is spiritual. Joy is awakened by and awakens the spirit. This is what makes it so special. The really wonderful thing about joy is that it is available to all. Joy is a spiritual experience that often results from doing something truly good or experiencing something good. It lifts a person out of his or her usual mundane, earthly experience and into the infinite, the eternal. Joy is the emotion of heavenly beings, and it is probably as close to the experience of heaven as we will ever have while here on earth.

"If you keep My commandments, you will abide in My love; just as I have kept My Father's commandments and abide in His love. These things I have spoken to you so that My joy may be in you, and that your joy may be made full" (John 15:10–11).[1]

Joy results when one connects with the transcendent, experiences God in one's life, or is reminded that there is truly more to life than just this material existence. It is a sacred emotion that is common among those of deep faith. Singing worship songs or praying together can elicit joy, so it is often linked with experiencing God within a community. Joy results when we abide in God's love, expressing that love to others in and outside of the faith community. This kind of love lifts us out of difficult circumstances to a higher place, gives us a different perspective, and enables us to live the full life that God originally intended.

Joy can also be experienced in nature. Watching a spectacular sunset or sunrise or looking into a star-filled night sky can give us an awareness of the Divine and thereby fill us with wonder and awe. Such transcendent experiences are often accompanied by joy.

Perhaps the surest way to experience joy is to do what the Creator instructed us to do—love God and love others. Someone once said that if you want to meet Jesus, walk along the path that Jesus would walk.

> *For I was hungry and you gave me something to eat, I was thirsty and you gave me something to drink, I was a stranger and you invited me in, I needed clothes and you clothed me, I was sick and you looked after me, I was in prison and you came to visit me.*

> (MATTHEW 25:35–37)

Joy is indeed a sacred emotion, one that is reserved for those special moments when, consciously or unconsciously, we come into contact with the Divine.

A kind heart is

a fountain of gladness,

making everything in its vicinity

freshen into smiles.

—WASHINGTON IRVING

How Kindness Results in Joy

Performing acts of kindness toward those in need and being kind in the way that one relates to others more generally convey joy because, as I pointed out before, here is where we connect directly with the Divine. As we express gentle, genuine, generous, loving kindness to God's children, we are rewarded by the sacred emotion of joy.

The story of Scrooge in *A Christmas Carol* makes this point clearly. Nothing can keep back the floodgates of joy from those who, without expectation of return, are kind and generous to others. Throughout his life, Scrooge kept and hoarded everything. He was never kind to others, but instead used people to gain and acquire more and more wealth. As a result, he lived a lonely and angry existence, completely contained within his own world of self-centeredness. In the last part of his life, though, after being visited by three apparitions from the past, the present, and the future, he was scared into learning a lesson— he learned the necessity of giving to others. You may recall that as he began to show kindness and generosity to others, his whole demeanor changed. He began dancing and shouting exuberantly in the streets. In one of the final lines of the story, he says, "Can this much joy be safe for one individual?"[1]

Yes, joy comes about naturally as a result of intentional acts of kindness. When I stop to be kind to a needy stranger in a respectful way, I feel joyful. When I intentionally look a colleague in the eye and pay him or her a sincere compliment (with no expectation of return), I experience joy. When I pray with someone who is suffering emotional or physical pain and treat him in a caring and compassionate way, I cannot help but feel joy.

Emerson said,

If you love and serve men, you cannot by any hiding or stratagem, escape the remuneration. Secret retributions are always restoring the level, when disturbed, of Divine justice. It is impossible to tilt the beam. All the tyrants and proprietors and monopolists of the world in vain set their shoulders to heave the bar. Settles forevermore the ponderous equator to its line, and man and mote and star and sun must range within it, or be pulverized by the recoil.[2]

Should there be any surprise that acts of kindness that connect us to others and to the Divine are followed by the sacred emotion of joy? If these acts bring us into contact with a little bit of heaven, this is exactly what we should expect. Consider the description of heaven in the book of Revelation:

Those who bring sunshine into the lives of others,

cannot keep it from themselves.

—James M. Barrie

Kindness, like a boomerang,

always returns.

—Author unknown

Alleluia! The reign of the Lord our God the Almighty has begun; let us be glad and joyful and give praise to God, because this is the time for the marriage of the Lamb. His bride is ready, and she has been able to dress herself in dazzling white linen, because her linen is made of the good deeds of the saints.

(REVELATION 19:7–8)

In heaven, there is constant joy and gladness and praise, and this joy is at least partly based on the good deeds of those who have lived on this earth and, may I venture, *are living* on this earth and being kind to those in need. Thus, all of heaven rejoices ever the greater when we are kind to others, and some of that joy filters down to us here on earth.

Love and kindness are never wasted.

They always make a difference.

They bless the one who receives them,

and they bless you, the giver.

—BARBARA DE ANGELIS

The Double Blessing

Kindness affects both the person being kind and the recipient of that kindness. One result is that the recipient of kindness has his or her needs met. That person is likely to feel grateful, cared about, and blessed by the kind person. Likewise, the person who is being kind experiences the joy of making a difference in another person's life in a good way. Thus, a double blessing occurs with each act of kindness. The spiritual blessings from kindness have been emphasized over and over again. Consider the following sayings:

Kind words can be short and easy to speak but their echoes are truly endless. —MOTHER TERESA

Deeds of kindness are equal in weight to all the commandments. —THE TALMUD

Kindness in words creates confidence.
Kindness in thinking creates profundity.
Kindness in giving creates love.

—LAO-TSE[1]

Although to my knowledge there has been no scientific research on kindness, I'm willing to bet that kindness has more than just spiritual benefits. These benefits likely extend also to the mental health of both the kind person and the recipient of kindness. A person who is experiencing sadness or anxiety or fear simply cannot continue to feel that way when he or she is being kind and experiencing the joy and fulfillment that naturally result. We may indeed have a treatment here for emotional disorders that doesn't have side effects and doesn't cost anything except time, intention, and goodwill. It is certainly the golden elixir that makes faulty relationships work better. How true is the comment by Albert Schweitzer, who said, "Constant kindness can accomplish much. As the sun makes ice melt, kindness causes misunderstanding, mistrust, and hostility to evaporate."

I wonder how often people would need antidepressants and psychotherapy if they started to be consistently kind to all those around them. This is not to underestimate the pain that depressive or anxiety disorders cause in people's lives, or to dismiss the need for medication or expert counseling in helping to relieve these disorders. Emotional problems almost always have genetic and biological causes that require medical treatments, just as do illnesses such as high blood pressure or diabetes. And sometimes people who have experienced a lot of emotional pain in life are the most compassionate, kind, and caring. Their own pain enables them to understand and feel for those who are needy and suffering. So, this issue is clearly not a simple one. However, my guess is that at whatever level of emotional distress a person is in, being consistently kind to others will help him or her feel better, even if it doesn't eliminate all of the painful feelings.

Besides better mental health, kind people may also experience physical health benefits. We know from a host of research studies that our emotions influence our physical bodies in many ways. Psychological stress can raise blood pressure, adversely affect the heart, interfere with immune function, and even cause our cells to prematurely age.[2] Anything that neutralizes that stress is likely to help protect or enhance those physiological systems that are impaired by stress. Thus, it is only logical that acts of kindness might not only improve mental health but boost physical health as well. There is at least preliminary evidence that those who do good deeds for others actually have measurably better health and live longer too.[3]

Those who are the receivers of kindness also appear to experience both emotional and physical health benefits. Scientific studies show that people who report higher "social support" have greater well-being, less depression, better physical health, and greater longevity.[4] Thus, being kind to others blesses the total health (physical, emotional, and spiritual) of both the giver and the receiver in ways that researchers are only now beginning to discover.

When I was young,

I used to admire intelligent people;

as I grow older, I admire kind people.

—Abraham Joshua Heschel,

Jewish theologian

Treat everyone

with politeness,

even those who are rude to you—

not because they are nice,

but because you are.

—AUTHOR UNKNOWN

When Joy Doesn't Result

Sometimes when you are kind to another person, joy doesn't follow. This will be very disappointing and discouraging. When it happens, you must reexamine your intentions. Are your intentions only for the good of the other person, or are you hoping to get something (even joy)?[1] I learned in my psychiatric training that the mind can be very deceptive and may conceal from us our real motivations. Thus, we may quickly justify our actions as solely for the benefit of others, when in reality we may have an underlying desire to benefit in some way. In its purest form, kindness expects nothing in return and is not upset when the recipient gives nothing back. Kindness is its own reward.

The flower of kindness will grow.

Maybe not now, but it will some day.

And in kind that kindness will flow,

for kindness grows in this way.

—ROBERT ALAN

Even when intentions are pure, however, joy may not result. When we seek to do good for another person and our actions are not welcomed or are perhaps misinterpreted, we may feel bad. If acts of kindness are unappreciated, negative emotions may follow. Being human, we all want some kind of positive response from the person to whom we've been kind. But that doesn't always happen. If appreciation doesn't follow, most of the time there is a reason why the recipient of our kindness isn't grateful. That reason usually relates to our not knowing the person well enough to understand what his or her needs truly are. The sick and dependent person in a wheelchair whom we offer to push down the hall may be upset and angry over being in a wheelchair and needing such help. Any help given may simply reinforce feelings of dependency and loss of control. In such situations, our acts of kindness become irritating and resented rather than appreciated.

Of course, sometimes the person to whom we are kind is simply rude. Perhaps the person expects or feels entitled to such treatment. Perhaps he or she is just angry at the world in general, and the person offering kindness may be a safe target. Usually, however, persistent acts of kindness and goodwill eventually wear down that anger or rudeness, eventually resulting in gratitude and thankfulness. How long this takes will depend on the person and the amount of psychological baggage he or she is carrying. If repeated acts of kindness (done with full knowledge of the person's actual needs) still elicit no appreciation, at some point it may be necessary to gently and tactfully confront the person about his or her behavior. Before doing this, though, be sure you thoroughly understand the person's circumstances and needs as he or she perceives them.

Finally, growth in maturity requires that acts of kindness be done not simply to experience a feeling, but for other ultimately more important reasons. Such acts should not be dependent on a particular emotion. It is not surprising that often in life we must do things not because they feel good, but because they are the right things to do—because they are good. The payoff of practicing kindness over time is that it settles the habit of gently and sensitively loving others into our way of acting and being in the world, independent of any particular result. This, of course, is our ultimate goal and a valuable target to shoot for. None of us is perfect, however, and emotions are usually powerful motivations for behavior. Joy is so often a result of being kind to others that this is at least a place to start for the less mature of us (like me) and then, over time, maybe we will learn to perform kind acts for higher, more selfless reasons.

For what I do

is not the good

I want to do.

—Romans 7:19

Barriers to Kindness

I f kindness is a quality and characteristic of the Divine, if it is a true mark of a spiritual person, if it brings joy and blesses others, then why is it so hard to be kind? I struggle personally with this. Despite knowing its importance, being consistently and continuously kind to others is a great challenge for me. When we first start out with the idea of being kind, it comes easily. But as time passes, the newness begins to fade and we become less and less consistently kind. Why?

First, I think we are naturally inclined to focus on ourselves and our own needs, especially when life isn't going our way. When I feel good, loved, and successful in meeting my life goals, it is easy to be kind to others. When I'm in a bad mood or having trouble with my family or work, I become more focused on my own immediate needs. A powerful force within me constantly pulls me back to being self-serving. Evidently, my "lower nature" has a lot of control over me. It is a nature that we all struggle with, that has been with us our entire lives, and that will be with us for as long as we are here on earth. This nature is deeply ingrained, and often rules our actions and behavior.

For some reason, this is true even when we know that being kind to others is overwhelmingly in our best interests. It is like the war within that Paul talks about in his Letter to the Romans:

> *For I have the desire to do what is good, but I cannot carry it out. For what I do is not the good I want to do; no, the evil I do not want to do—this I keep on doing . . . For in my inner being I delight in God's law; but I see another law at work in the members of my body, waging war against the law of my mind and making me a prisoner . . .*
> (Romans 7:18–23)

Second, whenever we are hurt by or are in conflict with others, it is difficult to be kind. When we consciously intend to be kind and the person who is the object of our kindness rebuffs us or otherwise hurts our feelings, our anger immediately rises to cancel out any good feelings we may wish to project. This is perhaps most difficult when it applies to people closest to us, such as family. It is one thing to be kind to a stranger, which often involves only a few brief moments. It is quite another thing to be kind to those we love and live with in a continuing relationship. Loved ones have the ability to wound us and enrage us. That rage can stand in the way of kindness so that only a supreme act of will can overcome it, and there are not many of us with that kind of will power.

Third, whenever we're rushing to accomplish some worldly goal or task, being kind may be difficult. Being kind takes time and attention, and when both of those are in short supply, we will tend to forgo kindness. This is because our focus is on our own perceived need—to get a task or job done—not on the good of the other person. Unfortunately, it is a misdirected priority. Being kind should never come second.

Fourth, it is hard to be kind to someone you don't like, or who has repeatedly ignored or failed to respect you in the past. There are some individuals with whom we just don't mesh. Some people do or say things that rub us the wrong way. Perhaps they remind us of others in our past who have hurt or humiliated us. It is hard to be kind to these people. However, Jesus asked us to be kind even to our enemies:

> *You have heard that it was said, "Love your neighbor and hate your enemy." But I tell you: Love your enemies and pray for those who persecute you, that you may be sons of your Father in heaven . . . Be perfect, therefore, as your heavenly Father is perfect.*
>
> (MATTHEW 5:43–45, 48)

Perfection! A pretty high standard, I'd say. But why did Jesus encourage this? For *our* benefit. Being kind to an enemy makes us feel better, and may even convert that enemy into a friend. C. S. Lewis said, "The worldly man treats certain people kindly because he 'likes' them: the Christian, trying to treat every one kindly, finds himself liking more and more people as he goes on—including people he could not even have imagined himself liking at the beginning."

Fifth, it is difficult to be kind to people who are proud, self-confident, controlling, or in positions of authority. These people appear not to need our kindness. They may reject it outright or seek to capitalize on any kindness that we show to them. Being kind, as I mentioned earlier, does not mean allowing yourself to be used as a doormat or taken advantage of. It does not mean allowing others to push you around or have their own way because it takes too much effort for you to stand up for your rights. The kind person acts from a position

Be kind and compassionate

to one another,

forgiving each other,

just as in Christ God forgave you.

—EPHESIANS 4:32

of strength, authority, and choice. We have been given authority and commanded by our Creator to be kind. We then consciously choose to do so, even though we have the right and the freedom not to be kind.

So, are these barriers to kindness simply too much, too great to overcome? I certainly hope not. For some of us, perhaps for most of us, developing the quality of kindness may be one of the most important reasons why we are here on this earth. Indeed, some of us may spend the rest of our lives improving on our desire and ability to be consistently kind to others. Despite many retreats and lost ground, if we persist, I believe we will slowly, gradually, sometimes imperceptibly, move forward on this path of goodness. However, we must constantly remind ourselves of the goal and encourage each other as well to get back on the horse when we've been thrown off. I don't think we can do it alone and, thankfully, we don't have to. We have each other and the Big Guy that told us to do this in the first place.

Too often we underestimate

the power of a touch,

a smile, a kind word, a listening ear,

an honest compliment,

or the smallest act of caring,

all of which have the potential

to turn a life around.

—LEO BUSCAGLIA

Practicing Kindness

J ust as any other skill—playing a musical instrument, singing, or excelling at a sport—kindness needs to be practiced. While being kind is a very simple volitional act that anyone can do at any time, what is difficult is remembering to be kind and doing it. At least at the beginning, an effort must be made to keep the intention to be kind in conscious awareness. Although being kind comes natural to a few saints, for most of us, it does not. We will have to perform acts of kindness over and over again until they become a habit. It is only after they have become "second nature" for us that we will be able to be consistently kind.

What exactly is involved in being kind? Here are some ideas on how to practice being kind. Involve your whole person in this effort.

First, *listen*—actively listen and seek to understand the other person. Listening is the first and most important action of a kind person. Listening shows respect and honor for the other as an individual and for his or her unique needs—known only by that person. As the person talks, softly nod your head to acknowledge understanding and appreciation for what he or she is saying.

Second, *look* kind. In other words, put on a smile *appropriate to the situation*. Be careful with the smile, though, because the person who is hurting may misinterpret your smile as ridicule or making fun of them. Often it is more appropriate to have a concerned, caring look on your face than a smile. Also, look right into the eyes of the other person, unless you sense that this embarrasses him or her.

Third, *feel* kind. Conjure up a feeling of caring, love, and concern for the person and communicate it to him or her with your entire demeanor. If the person is sad or in distress, show serious concern. Try to match your emotional tone with that of the person to whom you are being kind. Remember, "Rejoice with those who rejoice; mourn with those who mourn" (Romans 12:15).

Fourth, *speak* kind words to the person. Be sure that they are simple and easy to understand and express your caring concern. Don't talk too much, though, because this can be burdensome for others. Remember that your caring presence is more important than what you say.

Fifth, if the situation calls for it, *touch* the person in an appropriate and kind way. Gently place your hand on the back of his or her hand, shoulder, or upper back. This may involve holding the person's hand or simply a light pat on the back, depending on how well you know the person. People

Always be

a little kinder

than necessary.

—JAMES M. BARRIE

who are suffering often feel lonely and isolated and need the caring touch of another human being. Occasionally, a person may not want to be touched, so be sensitive to that also and don't push it.

Sixth, *position* your body in a kind way, perhaps leaning forward in an interested and concerned manner. Try not to stand above the person and lean down over him or her, since this conveys an air of authority or superiority. Rather, get down on his or her level.

The more we practice kindness, the better we will be at it and the easier it will become. As American social writer Eric Hoffer said, "Kindness can become its own motive. We are made kind by being kind." Here are some practical ways that you can be kind to others.[1]

- Thank someone for something. Be sure that it is worthy of thanks and that your thanks is sincere.

- Compliment someone on his or her appearance or

attire (again, such a compliment should be based in reality, not simply flattery).

- Compliment someone for an action, attitude, or ability (speedy service, good job, thoughtfulness, solution to a problem, patience in a difficult situation).

- Write a kind note to the server at a restaurant (and accompany it with a generous tip).

- Hold the door open for someone.

- Send a card to someone to let him or her know how much he or she means to you.

- Tip someone for a service and look him or her right in the eye as you express thanks.

- Visit someone in a nursing home or hospital or a person who is homebound, and spend time listening to him or her.

- Give a hand to someone who is struggling with a physical problem (after asking if he or she wants help).

- Encourage someone who is having a hard time emotionally (but avoid giving advice).

- Stop and help a stranded motorist (if you are a man).

- Generously allow someone to merge into your lane in front of you.

- Forgive someone for something he or she has done to hurt you.

- Do the laundry or wash the dishes for your partner.

- Prepare a special dinner for your partner.

- Offer to watch your neighbors' pets when they are away on vacation.

- Show interest in something that excites someone else.

- Buy a coupon for two dinners and invite someone to join you.

- Buy tickets to a sporting event and invite someone to join you who likes the sport.

You may also try doing random acts of kindness anonymously (so that the other person cannot figure out who did it and cannot return the favor).[2]

- Send a helpful book, CD, or tape as a gift.

- Send flowers with an anonymous note saying something like: "From someone who respects and appreciates you."

- Put money in a parking meter if it looks as if the time is running out.

- Pay a highway toll for someone behind you or pay someone's grocery bill.

- Send money anonymously to someone in financial difficulty (include a kind note of encouragement).

- Tell an employer about someone who needs a job.

- Clean up after yourself (so that things are clean for the next person).

- Pick up someone else's trash and throw it away.

Try some of these acts of kindness. You may discover what reporter and philanthropist George Elliston did—"How beautiful a day can be when kindness touches it!"

I expect to pass through life but once.

If therefore,

there be any kindness I can show,

or any good thing I can do

to any fellow being,

let me do it now,

and not defer or neglect it,

as I shall not pass this way again.

—WILLIAM PENN

Being Kind to Strangers and Friends

D oing small acts of kindness for strangers is probably the best place to start for those trying to develop the habit of kindness since they are easier, take the least amount of time, and usually provide immediate gratification. Most people don't expect unknown people to be kind to them, so they are often surprised (and may even be a bit suspicious, thinking "What is this person's motive?"). Once they realize there is no "catch" and that you simply want to be helpful, most people are appreciative and grateful. Even just being friendly, courteous, and nice to strangers can be done in a kind and generous way, and will make you feel better. This is especially rewarding when you are traveling on business and away from friends and family.

Leslie Smith tells her story of an act of kindness and the positive experiences that resulted:

I was a traveling nurse (just recently stopped) and one of the most wonderful times in my life was when I was driving north for Christmas . . . I found a $20 bill and decided to put it to use . . . I paid for tolls for the people behind me and with that act of kindness—many smiles were brought to others' faces as well as mine . . . some people caught up with me and waved thank you, some had cars full of kids and presents and the waves made my day . . . so random acts of kindness are wonderful and brought smiles to many people that day . . . the most fun was trying to get the toll takers to do it . . . they looked at me as if I had lost my mind when I said—I would like to pay the toll for the 3 people behind me . . . but some of them really got into it . . . it is a special memory and one I hold in my heart every day.[1]

Being kind to friends who are well known to us is a little harder, but at least as rewarding as being kind toward strangers. The reason these people are our friends is probably because we have already been kind to them in one way or another. Some degree of kindness is usually expected from close friends, or they may feel obliged to return the favor in some way, so these acts may not be followed immediately by the appreciation a stranger might show. However, we should persist in acts of kindness toward friends and, if possible, take these acts to a new and higher level of frequency and effort. Friends will ultimately notice the change and will respond positively. Greater kindness on your part will almost always strengthen your relationships.

Beth Fryer tells the following story that illustrates kindness toward friends:

Once, many years ago, my mom was diagnosed with breast cancer and was scheduled for a mastectomy. That morning I attended a college class in which the husband of a good friend was also a student. Most mornings we said hello to one another and that was about it—he would sit with his guy friends, and I usually sat alone. When he entered class that morning, he came and sat next to me. He never mentioned my mom, never talked about the situation at all . . . he just sat next to me and chatted a bit. That was the day I learned that sometimes the kindest act is just to BE there . . . and I always remember this as one of the most touching acts of kindness I've ever received.[2]

When is a good time to start being kind to strangers or friends? When asked this question, Ralph Waldo Emerson responded: "You cannot do a kindness too soon, for you never know how soon it will be too late." So start immediately—with the person sitting next to you on the airplane, subway, or bus,[3] with the person standing in line with you at the grocery store, or with friends at school, work, or church.

You can't live a perfect day

without doing something

for someone who

will never be able to repay you.

—JOHN WOODEN

Be kind.

Everyone you meet is

fighting a hard battle.

—PHILO, GREEK PHILOSOPHER

Being Kind at Work

During our lifetimes, most of us spend at least eight hours a day, five days a week for fifty years, at work. This calculates out to nearly one hundred thousand hours (seventeen years of awake time). During work, we are constantly interacting with colleagues, clients, and customers. How we treat the people we work with will largely determine the quality of our lives during this huge block of time. It will also determine and reflect our character, how others view us, and the impact we have on their lives. Being kind to others at work is the secret to the success, joy, and satisfaction that we experience on the job. Below is a story about how a physician's kindness affected the life of his patient.

Dr. Thomas James, a family physician in Illinois, was making rounds to check on the status of five patients who had been hospitalized that week. He was not excited about the next room he had to go into. This was Room 208, Mrs. Jane Brown's room. Mrs. Brown had a number of chronic medical conditions that were interfering with her ability to live independently and care for herself at home, and none of the conditions were responding very well to treatment. A proud and independent woman all of her life, she was now confined to bed and angry over her increasing dependency on others. She was also disappointed with her health care professionals for their lack of success in treating the myriad of illnesses that were interfering with her ability to walk. During previous visits, she had been very demanding with Dr. James, and seemed to show little appreciation for the efforts he and his team were making to determine the cause of her disability. Before entering the room, Tom told himself that despite how he felt toward Mrs. Brown, he needed to be kind to her even if she said something rejecting and hurtful. Taking a deep breath, he knocked on the door, opened it, and walked in.

Looking directly into Mrs. Brown's eyes, he greeted her with a serious and concerned expression on his face and came to her bedside. He pulled up a chair, sat down in it, and said, "I hear it was a rough night, Mrs. Brown," continuing to look gently and directly into her eyes. She quickly shot back, "You don't know how bad it was, doctor. Can't you give me anything to help me sleep and relax?" Tom responded, "Let me look at your medicines and see what I can do. I can't guarantee anything, but there may be something without a lot of side effects that could help you rest better at night." He continued, "Besides the problem sleeping, how are you doing otherwise? Do you think you're making progress?" "No doctor, I don't," said Mrs. Brown. "You'd think you doctors would be able to do

Kindness is the language which

the deaf can hear

and the blind can see.

—MARK TWAIN

something to get me back on my feet, but nobody seems to take my complaints seriously."

"I take your complaints seriously, Mrs. Brown," said Dr. James in a non-defensive tone, maintaining a concerned look on his face. "We're doing a number of tests and should have some answers this afternoon. For now, let's talk about the most important concern that you have this morning. Do you have one that outranks all the others?" "Well, doctor," said Mrs. Brown with some hesitation, "My daughter hasn't visited me a single time since I was admitted to the hospital five days ago. I can't believe it. I'm so hurt." "Tell me more," said Tom, nodding his head slightly up and down in an understanding way while giving her his full and undivided attention.

Mrs. Brown spent the next five minutes telling Dr. James about the problems she was having with her daughter, and how her daughter seemed not to care about her anymore. "She is my only daughter, doctor. How could she treat me this way?" "I don't know, Mrs. Brown, but this conflict with your daughter seems to be bothering you a great deal. What do you think would help you resolve these problems the two of you are having?" Mrs. Brown went on to say how discouraged she was because she really didn't know what to do. Dr. James said, "I will help you figure out a plan. Would you allow me to do that?" After a pause while she carefully scrutinized his face, Mrs. Brown responded, "Yes, doctor. Although I don't know how you can help. But thank you." Dr. James leaned forward and took her hand gently into his, saying quietly, "Okay. We'll both think about this on our own and discuss what we come up with this afternoon. In the meantime, I will check your chart and be sure that you have something ordered to help you rest at night. Goodbye for now, Mrs. Brown," he said, again looking directly into her eyes with a caring smile and giving her hand a firm but gentle squeeze before getting up and leaving the room.

Although we are not all physicians, each of us has a job that we work at (whether that job involves work inside or outside of the home) and people with whom we must interact on that job. We face the same challenge as Dr. James. Will we be kind to those with whom we work? Will we be able to continue to be kind even when work gets tough and everybody else around us is giving us a hard time?

Kindness is the life's blood,

the elixir of marriage.

Kindness makes the difference

between passion and caring.

Kindness is tenderness.

Kindness is love, but perhaps greater than love . . .

Kindness is good will.

Kindness says, "I want you to be happy."

Kindness comes very close

to the benevolence of God.

—RANDOLPH RAY,

MY LITTLE CHURCH AROUND THE CORNER

Being Kind to Family

I sn't it a strange thing that the people we have the most difficulty being kind to are the people we love and depend on the most? But it is true. It is easy to be kind to a stranger whom we don't know and whom we may not have much contact with. Family members know us the best, especially our weaknesses and faults. We spend most of our time with our family and often must compromise our life choices to appease them. This makes being kind to family on a daily basis the ultimate challenge. The benefits of such kindness, however, are probably greater and more direct than being kind to anyone else.

Take Sally, for example. She is like many Americans today. Sally is a middle-aged housewife with a teenage son in high school and a daughter in the fifth grade. Her husband works in the construction business, and they live in a middle-class neighborhood in the suburbs of a moderate-sized city. To help make ends meet, she works part time as a substitute teacher in her daughter's grammar school. Sally's father died a couple of years ago of cancer, and her mother, Lee, is still alive but getting older, feebler, and having more health problems. Recently, she moved in with Sally's family, since it was becoming evident that it was not safe for her to continue living alone. This was stressful for Lee, since she didn't like living in someone else's home and being a burden on them. It was also stressful on Sally and her family because her mother could not be left alone safely by herself and was often grumpy.

Over the years, however, Sally had made kindness a habit. She was motivated to do so by her religious beliefs, which emphasized "Love thy neighbor." She decided to make an active effort to be kinder after hearing a sermon at church one

Sunday. Sally thought that a good place to start would be to practice being kind to members of her own family. When she first tried to do this, it was not easy. Her husband and kids were constantly doing things that got on her nerves. She would have to decide with great effort that she would say something kind to one family member each day, and rotate this "chore" between family members. After doing this for a while, she noticed that her family began to respond to her. This greatly encouraged Sally to continue saying kind things and acting in a kind way. There were times, however, when Sally and her husband were at odds over something, when it just seemed impossible to be kind to him. At those times, he rejected her acts of kindness, often based on sheer willpower, which really hurt and made her angry.

Sally persisted, though, and over time, she began to see more and more positive results. Besides, she felt so much better about herself whenever she was kind. This encouraged her enough so she decided she would say kind things at least once a day to each member of her family. After a while, Sally noticed that being kind was becoming easier and easier, so much so that she would say or do kind things several times a day to each family member.

She had relapses, though. If she was having a bad day or if there was conflict in the family, it was so hard to say or do something kind. At the end of the day, she would discover that she hadn't been kind to anyone in her family, and this made her feel bad. Sally felt like a failure on such days.

Nevertheless, she was determined. Being kind just seemed like the "right" thing to do, and if she just didn't give up, Sally believed that good things would result. She was at least trying to love her neighbor, which her minister and her Bible said was important. So, even when her acts of kindness weren't reciprocated or appreciated, Sally felt that she was at least obeying God.

After a time, especially as she became more and more accustomed to it, saying kind things and acting in a kind manner toward her husband and kids began to pay off. The arguments with her husband occurred less and less frequently, and they both got over them quicker. There were fewer conflicts with her teenage son, who would occasionally be kind to her in return (which really surprised her!). Sally's relationship with her daughter also improved. She noticed that her daughter was opening up more and more, which made her feel really good.

Just as things began to improve within her immediate family, however, Sally now had her mother to deal with. This was really hard. The burden of working during the day, caring for her family, and ensuring that her mother got bathed, dressed, and didn't fall or hurt herself, was almost too much for Sally. Furthermore, her kindness didn't seem to work with her mother as well as it had with other family members. Lee was so

The more sympathy you give,

the less you need.

—Malcolm S. Forbes

upset and angry at leaving her home and now having to be helped with everything that she didn't appreciate anything that Sally did for her.

As Sally began to feel more and more irritable over the strain, her kindness toward other family members began to lessen. It was just too hard to be kind to someone who didn't respond and in fact resented her kindness. Again, however, Sally did not give up. Despite not feeling one bit like being kind to her mother, she again decided that she would say or do something kind at least once a day to her mother, no matter how she felt or how Lee responded. Sally remembered that it had taken quite some time before her other family members responded to her acts of kindness, so she decided that she could not give up on her mother. In the sermon that had changed her life many years before, Sally's pastor had quoted the great English poet, Samuel Johnson, who said, "Kindness is in our power, even when fondness is not."

She decided on a plan. Each morning when she heard her mother wake up and begin to stir about in her bedroom, Sally would knock on the door, enter the room, and give her mother a gentle hug (holding on for a few seconds longer than usual). At the end of the hug, she would say, "Good morning, Mother, I love you." After helping her mother get dressed, Sally would fix breakfast for her and for any family members who happened to be around. On weekends when Sally was home with her mother, she would sit down next to Lee for a couple of minutes and place a hand on her mother's knee, often not saying anything. When she spoke to her mother, she would try to look her directly in the eyes, "soften" her look, and put on a kind smile. During these times and others, Sally tried to treat her mother with respect and honor. When her mother needed help with something, Sally asked her how she could help and took directions from her on what to do (if reasonable). She would give her mother options when something had to be done so that Lee felt like she had choices. At bedtime, she would put her mother to bed, say a little prayer with her, give her a hug, and tell her again that she loved her.

At first, Lee resisted these actions. But after weeks of persistence on Sally's part, Lee's resistance weakened and she became more responsive. The coldness began to give way to reciprocal acts of kindness—Lee began to hug Sally back, place her hand on her daughter's hand, and became more cooperative in other ways as well. Once again, Sally's determination to be kind was paying off.

No kind action ever stops with itself.

One kind action leads to another.

Good example is followed.

A single act of kindness

throws out roots in all directions,

and the roots spring up and make new trees.

The greatest work that

kindness does to others is that

it makes them kind themselves.

—AMELIA EARHART

Helping Others Experience the Joy of Kindness

Nearly 2,500 years ago, Sophocles (447 B.C.) remarked, "Kindness it is that brings forth kindness always." When we are kind to others, this motivates them to be kind to others in return. This is what I think is really exciting about the results of kindness. Our acts of kindness are like tossing a rock in a pond and watching the ripples go out from the center. We may not always be able to see those ripples, but they are going out from that initial impact, out through the entire pond.

One of the best things we can do for others is to encourage them to be kind and show them how to do it. This will bring joy into their lives, and will do much more for them than our simply meeting their immediate needs. Of course, you can't lecture people about kindness and expect to get anywhere. Kindness is something that must come from the heart. People have to want to be kind.

People need the experience of seeing the results of kindness so that they will want to be kind themselves. When they sense the joy and fulfillment that we have when we are kind to others, they will want to have those feelings too. However, that may not be enough for some. They may also need to feel what it is like to be a receiver of kindness to fully appreciate the benefit of such actions. When someone is kind to us, our natural response is to want to pay that person back or, if that is not possible, to be kind to someone else in return. Thus, for most people, it probably requires both seeing how being kind affects us and also experiencing what it is like to be on the receiving end of that kindness. I have told my 17-year-old many times how important it is to be kind to others. Unless he actually sees me being kind to others, and unless I am kind to him, those words will be wasted.

Most of us also need encouragement. Developing into a kind person is not an easy task. There will be many times when joy does not occur, despite our best attempts to be kind to others. Some of us may have the ability to delay gratification by knowing that whether rewarded or not, repeated acts of kindness will help us to become better people in the long run. Others need reminders and encouragement. Let us support one another in being kind. It may be useful to enter into a formal pact with a friend and agree to hold each other accountable to being kind to others. Every so often, more frequently at the beginning, have a meeting or telephone call with that friend, report your successes and failures, and inquire about his or hers. This is one sure way to sustain progress in being kind.

Kindness is

the greatest wisdom.

—AUTHOR UNKNOWN

Conclusion

I n this little book, you have learned a lot about what kindness is, the joy that results from being kind, and how to practice and develop the habit of kindness when relating to strangers, friends, co-workers, and family. I have learned a lot too.

Kindness is a gentle form of love. When kind to others, we demonstrate the very best of what it means to be human. It takes practice, persistence, patience, and wisdom, and seldom comes without a price. But it has a big payoff. It is truly a full life that kind and caring people live. Kindness nourishes the mind, the body, and the spirit of both the giver and the receiver. It is an opportunity to act in a way that is essentially and ultimately Divine.

The question is, What will we do with all this knowledge? Will we now go out and be kind to others and develop a consistent habit of kindness that will transform our lives? Will we encourage others to be kind by word and deed, and support them in their own efforts? Or will we try a few times and then fall back into our old and comfortable self-centered ways? That is the challenge that remains before us. I, for one, will give it a shot. Will you?

Notes

The Divine Love

1. *The Holy Bible* (Chicago: Catholic Bible Publishers, 1969).

2. Ibid.

3. Adapted from Christopher Ian Chenoweth, "The Day of Christ's Great Commandment," *Positive Christianity Daily Inspiration*, dailyinspiration@sonic.sparklist.com, April 13, 2006.

Joy—The Sacred Emotion

1. New American Standard Bible (NAS) (La Habra, CA: Foundation Publications, 2001).

How Kindness Results in Joy

1. Adapted from Christopher Ian Chenoweth, "Giving Yourself Away," *Positive Christianity Daily Inspiration*, http://sonic.sparklist.com/scripts/lyris.pl?visit=dailyinspiration&id=306009297, April 19, 2006.

2. Ralph Waldo Emerson, *Lectures and Biographical Sketches* (Boston: Houghton-Mifflin, 1883), 186.

The Double Blessing

1. Lao-Tse, considered the first philosopher of the Taoist school, wrote *Te-Tao Ching,* one of the most sacred texts of Taoism. From http://www.wisdomquotes.com/cat_kindness.html.

2. E. S. Epel, E. H. Blackburn, J. Lin, F. S. Dhabhar, N. E. Adler, J. D. Morrow, and R. M. Cawthon, "Accelerated Telomere Shortening in Response to Life Stress," *Proceedings of the National Academy of Sciences* 101, no. 49 (2004):17312–15.

3. S. L. Brown, R. M. Nesse, A. D. Vinokur, and D. M. Smith, "Providing Social Support May Be More Beneficial Than Receiving It: Results from a Prospective Study of Mortality," *Psychological Science* 14, no. 4 (2003): 320–27.

4. J. S. House, K. R. Landis, and D. Umberson, "Social Relationships and Health," *Science* 241 (1988): 540–45.

When Joy Doesn't Result

1. Joy is often the natural result of acts of kindness; however, if acts of kindness are done specifically with the goal of joy in mind, rather than to help the other person, joy is unlikely to result.

Practicing Kindness

1. Some of these have been adapted from G. Grant, *100 Kindnesses*, glgc.com/kindness/100.html.

2. Some of these have been adapted from: Z. Pliskin, *Kindness: Changing People's Lives for the Better* (New York: Mesorah Publications, 2000).

Being Kind to Strangers and Friends

1. Rebecca Ryan Resources, Story 13, *Random Acts of Kindness Edition with 33 Heartfelt "Stories of Kindness,"* http://www.intouchmag.com/33kindnessstories2.html.

2. Ibid., Story 3.

3. In most cases, for safety and appropriateness, it is probably wise to restrict personal interactions with strangers to those of the same sex.

Resources on Kindness

For Adults

Barnes, Emilie. *If Teacups Could Talk: Sharing a Cup of Kindness With Treasured Friends*. Eugene, OR: Harvest House Publishers, 2003.

Brown, Gail, Nancy Zieman, and Nancy Luedtke. *Creative Kindness: People and Projects Making a Difference and How You Can, Too*. Iola, WI: KP Books, 2003.

Green, Terri. *Simple Acts of Kindness: Practical Ways to Help People in Need.*Grand Rapids, MI: Revell, 2004.

Gulley, Philip. *Hometown Tales: Recollections of Kindness, Peace and Joy.* San Francisco: HarperSanFrancisco, 2001.

Forrest, Margot Silk. *A Short Course in Kindness: A Little Book on the Importance of Love and the Relative Unimportance of Just About Everything Else.*Cayucos, CA: L. M. Press, 2003.

Lagana, Laura, and Tom Lagana. *Serving Time, Serving Others: Acts of Kindness by Inmates, Prison Staff, Victims, and Volunteers*. Georgetown, DE: Fruit-Bearer Publishing, 2003.

Lovasik, Lawrence G. *The Hidden Power of Kindness: A Practical Handbook for Souls, Who Dare to Transform the World, One Deed at a Time*. Manchester, NH: Sophia Institute Press, 1999.

Markova, Dawna, introduction, and Daphne Rose Kingma, foreword. *Random Acts of Kindness.* Rev. ed. York Beach, ME: Conari Press, 2002.

Pliskin, Zelig. *Kindness: Changing People's Lives for the Better.* New York: Mesorah Publications, Ltd, 2000.

Ruggiero, Vincent Ryan. *The Practice of Loving Kindness: A Guide to Spiritual Fulfillment and Social Harmony.* Hyde Park, NY: New City Press, 2003.

Salzberg, Sharon. *The Force of Kindness: Change Your Life with Love & Compassion,* book and compact disc set. Boulder, CO: Sounds True, 2005.

Sjogren, Steve. *Conspiracy of Kindness: A Refreshing Approach to Sharing the Love of Jesus with Others,* 10th Anniv. Ed. Ventura, CA: Regal Books, 2003.

The Power of Kindness for Teens: True Stories Written by Teens for Teens from the Pages of Guideposts. Nashville, TN: Ideals Publications, 2004.

For Kids

BOOKS

Hollenbeck, Kathleen M. *Teaching with Favorite Clifford Books: Great Activities Using 15 Books about Clifford the Big Red Dog—That Build Literacy and Foster Cooperation and Kindness.* New York: Instructor Books, 2001.

Markova, Dawna, introduction, and Rosalyn Carter, foreword. *Kids' Random Acts of Kindness.* York Beach, ME: Conari Press, 1994.

Paley, Vivian Gussin. *The Kindness of Children.* Cambridge, MA: Harvard University Press, 2000.

VIDEOS

Mister Rogers' Neighborhood: Kindness. Prince Tuesday's new teacher gives King Friday a lesson in generosity and politeness.
http://www.answers.com/topic/mister-rogers-neighborhood-kindness

Sharing and Kindness. Two stories that share the importance of kindness to others. http://www.erckids.com/detail.asp?id=3729&media=2